DIRECTIONS HOME

DIRECTIONS HOME

by Ricky Hopkins, Sr.

CONTENTS

PREFACE

As a real estate and community engagement professional, a greater need was identified with many first time homebuyers. The need is not confined to a certain generation, but somewhat rooted in a general misunderstanding of the fundamentals of dollars and sense. The general purpose of this book is to motivate, explain and encourage the home buying process and the benefits thereafter. All information expressed herein is designed and formatted to outline the standard layout of the purchasing process. This book will address many curiosities, terminologies and questions that are relative. The first time home buyer will gain understanding of the complete process. They will be prepared to achieve the American Dream of home ownership with confidence, knowledge and great expectations.

One of my objectives with this book is to connect the dots in terms of explaining how being a homeowner ties into wealth building and retirement planning. This may be a no brainer to many—but not all. Understanding the educational component of being a homeowner is just as important as enjoying the bundle of rights that comes along with it. Many people are impeded as a result of the lack of knowledge. My hope is that this book helps innumerable people and I will continue to share my knowledge and wisdom with the world.

Chapter 1

WHY HOMEOWNERSHIP?

Let's first understand what homeownership is and the benefits thereof. Homeownership puts you in the driver seat of life vs. the back seat. When you shift from non-homeowner to homeowner, what does this really mean? You will acquire fee simple ownership which gives the homeowner all legal rights to do as they wish with their land, including improvements; as long as no laws are being broken nor any zoning and/or ordinances are being violated. There are no landlords to answer to, regarding permissions of any kind. As long as the terms of your mortgage remain compliant, you have no one to answer to other than yourself.

 Once you become a homeowner, you instantly become an "unofficial" committee member and voice within that community. There's a natural camaraderie and gravity amongst homeowners. Homeowners depend on each other from a vested perspective to maintain, beautify, preserve and protect the ascent and sustainability of their community. They realize the importance and benefits of a walkable and desirable community. Establishing friendships with neighbors can prove beneficial to all in many ways. So remember that a happy, healthy and cohesive community creates a desirable, peaceful, sustainable and pleasant community.

Once you purchase a home, you've now consumed the largest portion of life also known as the American Dream of homeownership. Homeownership literally puts you in the game of life and helps you to prioritize and live your life as intended. You can enjoy the tax benefits, accruing equity, making improvements and learning more about the inheritable aspect of becoming a homeowner. One last noteworthy thing to remember regarding owning a home, is that mortgage payments can be less than rent payments.

❖

Chapter 2

LET'S TALK CREDIT

Having great credit is powerful and often underestimated by many. A standard definition of credit is simply an agreement for something borrowed or financed with an obligation to be paid back later under a said set of terms. There are many reasons why a person would want and need to have great credit. It is needed to establish your creditworthiness, trust and legitimacy within the credit world. It can certainly be viewed as the "master key" in opening doors to the wide world of lending. It's critical that an obligator stays compliant with any credit agreements. Defaulting on credit obligations can result in huge regret and leave you financially wounded.

Let's discuss credit from a FICO score point of view. Your FICO score is typically a three digit number derived from the activity within your credit report that will determine the risks of granting you credit and at what cost. It is critical that you understand the power of having great credit. Your FICO score speaks the loudest and carries the most weight. The common components that make up your FICO score are payment history, outstanding credit card balances, history, credit type and inquiries. Your FICO score is a snapshot of your credit profile and does not take into account any personal situations or hardships.

Your credit score is going to be the largest factor in determining whether or not you will qualify for a home loan. There is no universal score that lenders use to pre-qualify all prospective borrowers. Some lenders have the ability and discretion to work with various credit scores as they deem compliant. They will look at other adjoining factors such as debt to income ratio, income tax history, employment history, and other things relative. For Example, one lender may pre approve an FHA borrower with a credit score of 580 if the other factors are good. We may try another lender with the same client and get rejected. There are so many risks, regulations and discretions to consider within the qualification process. We must remain mindful of underwriting assessments as it pertains to the risk analysis. A loan denial may occur for various reasons, even if your credit score is acceptable. There could be debt-to-income ratio issues or lack of adequate funds on hand to close the deal—just to name a couple.

There are some cases where stated or acquired income may not be "qualifiable." Bankruptcies and excessive student loan debt could become pertinent issues as well.

Mortgage lending is a diligent process and timeliness on all sides is crucial. A loan officer can pull credit at any time within that process if it is required within their scope of work. Many prospective home buyers may not be aware of secondary credit searches that can be performed subsequent to loan pre-approval. This search could potentially reveal any hidden government/federal defaults that may not initially show up on your credit report. This secondary search is more common with FHA insured loans given they are federally insured and government backed. This can spell disaster for your home loan that's in progress if not discovered soon enough. If you have any IRS, student loan issues or the like, be sure to get them resolved before entering into the home buying process.

Approximately 75% of all credit reports have some type of error on them. A corrected error on a credit report may increase a credit score tremendously; given the magnitude of the error. The best thing to do is stay knowledgeable about what's on your credit report and to identify any errors. Whether the errors are simply misinformation, non-compliant or typographical, they should be corrected. If derogatory credit becomes an issue, it is recommended to seek professional, reputable credit counseling.

Chapter 3

DO I HAVE THE ABILITY TO PURCHASE?

This question weighs heavily on the minds of many prospective home buyers. Perhaps, this may be the most significant question; whether you have the ability to purchase now or at a future date—your dream of becoming a home owner can be achieved. Sadly, there are far too many people who continue to defer their dreams of home ownership or who may have written it off altogether.

As a first time homebuyer, having the right mindset is critical. Many prospective, first time homebuyers fall victim to false and bloated information. This is avoidable by performing a quick self-assessment prior to reaching out to a real estate agent or loan officer. Here are the steps:

- Obtain and view a current copy of your credit report to assure score and accuracy

- Review debt to income ratio

- Maintain proper year-to-year tax filings

- Savings account balance that meets the need for down-payment and closing costs

Keep in mind that there's no hit to a credit report if pulled by the debtor. Credit counseling may or may not be needed. If your credit report and fico score checks out as good then you've just hurdled pass more than half the battle that hinders or prevents a pre-approval from being issued.

Your pre-approved amount will be determined once you connect with a loan officer and complete a credit application, in addition to pulling a credit report.

It's all about creditworthiness.

There are a few ways to you can go about connecting with a lender:

- ⇨ Speak with someone at your current banking institution

- ⇨ Ask for a referral from a friend, real estate agent or net working connections

A seasoned real estate agent typically will have a trustworthy network that could prove helpful.

However, One disclaimer that's worthy of mentioning is that all lenders and lending institutions are not created equal. Pre-approval for a home loan can vary from lender to lender, given underwriting discretion and HUD guidelines. Lending is not a "one size fit all" industry. Working with a seasoned real estate agent prior to seeking pre-approval is advantageous. Your real estate agent should sit down with you to discuss your individual needs and specific requirement for your real estate journey. This process will prepare you to seek out the lender that's right for you. The next step is to begin exploring first time homebuyer assistance, interest rates, financing options and much more.

Timeliness and efficiency will work in your favor when working with your lender of choice. They will begin the approval process upon receipt of all requested documentation, including the credit application. You're typically notified with your results whether pre-approved or denied shortly thereafter. If the lender is unable to issue a pre-approval, the actionable next steps are clarified. The first is to determine why and the second is to begin repairing whatever needs to be fixed. A loan denial from one institution may not be the end as they are not universal. Over the course of my real estate career I've witnessed several borrowers get a denied pre-approval from one lending institution only to get approved with another. It's critical to have a seasoned real estate team to assist you with this process to avoid becoming discouraged, frustrated or perhaps even cheated out of your dream. A great loan officer should always follow up the denial with a reason and a remedy so the homebuyer can continue to feel encouraged and hopeful.

Chapter 4

RENT PAYMENTS VS. MORTGAGE PAYMENTS

Renting is simply an agreement between owner and tenant to use owner's property for a said period for regular payment. The terms "rent" and "lease" are practically interchangeable. The short difference between the two is just simply time or duration period. The term "lease" can simply indicate a longer period of time.

Renting is necessary in some short term situations but certainly shouldn't be the long term objective. There are many things to consider when looking at renting vs. owning. Becoming a home owner provides many significant benefits to the thing called "life." Some of these benefits will aid in retirement planning, savings, testate plans, bundle of rights, free and clear goals and equity building just to name a few. These are some of the largest benefits that come along with becoming a home owner.

When we look at the contrast between rent vs. mortgage, more than likely it will be cheaper to own vs. rent. Being a home owner enables you to enjoy your bundle of rights paired with benefitting from the accumulation of your home's year-to-year equity. This equity can contribute significantly to ones retirement. Accumulating equity in your home is a lifeline and makes for a significant and viable savings over time.

A mortgage is a security instrument for a debt that's owed on your home. The home itself serves as collateral. Your monthly mortgage is actually paying down a debt. This mortgage will allow you to own the largest purchase of your life and to acquire your largest inheritable asset. You will never own a home with a simple rental agreement in place. This is why time is of the essence. You wouldn't want to spend the bulk of your life renting only to miss out on your largest and most significant asset which is home ownership.

There are more fundamental disadvantages of renting that we can high-light. As a renter, you will never possess the right of a grantor. There are no tax advantages and you can be subject to a thirty day notice to vacate.

You have to acquire permissions from the landlord for any upgrades or modifications. The greatest disadvantage may be the fact that your rent payments aren't contributing in any way towards your retirement nor savings. Maintaining a good payment history and good tenancy can contribute to a positive recommendation and a positive line item on your credit report. However, it has to be reported by the landlord.

Chapter 5

HOW TO CHOOSE
A REAL ESTATE AGENT

The vast majority of prospects in need of a real estate agent will acquire that agent through practical means. They will use a referral from a friend or family member, an agent discovered on social media or someone they've crossed paths with. Some people will just simply call into a real estate office and connect whomever answers the phone. Whichever option applies to you in choosing an agent, just know that a real estate agent is not "a one size fit all."

Real agents have varying degrees of knowledge, niches, experience and drive. Many real estate agents even have specialized areas in which they have chosen to represent and master. Some agents may opt to work as listing agents only, some as buyer's only, or some may choose to work in a team setting. Be sure to learn more about your agent of choice as they learn more about you as their client.

A first time home buyer should understand the importance of having a consultation. This meeting between client and real estate agent is imperative to assess the compatibility of the agency. Both parties should walk away feeling encouraged and connected. While it is not mandatory, it is recommended that at least three real estate agents are interviewed. A great agent should possess the ability to not only impressively answer questions, but to relay just as much remarkable information. Having the knowledge to explain the market to the buyer client regarding their price range should be done inclusively.

Real estate agents should speak to their clients about the acronym D.U.S.T. upon every consultation. This acronym stands for desirability, utility, scarcity and transferability. It affects all things real estate and real property values. These four elements measure the overall desirability of the property. Be sure to speak more about D.U.S.T. with your real estate agent.

Choosing a real estate agent is certainly something that shouldn't be taken lightly, given all that's on the line. You should develop a level of trust in the agent you choose and be careful not to seek information from others outside of the team. An agency between buyer and agent can go left quickly and become contentious if the client listens more to others rather than their agent. This can cause a breakdown and regret on all sides within the agency.

Avoid listening to other people and trust the agent you chose to represent you. The experience of an agent matters greatly. Real estate entails negotiating skills, strategizing and understanding real estate contracts and forms. Your agent's ability to identify and understand market trends, ethics, cooperation, data and home values are critical. Choosing the best agent for you and your unique needs can certainly make this journey all that it is meant to be. A great real estate agent can assure your best interest and provide you with an amazing and unforgettable home buying experience.

Chapter 6

HOW YOUR REAL ESTATE TEAM SHOULD LOOK

You may be scratching your head and wondering what team? Your real estate agent is the team's captain. Your essential team consists of your real estate agent, loan officer, home inspector and title company. Keep in mind there are various reasons that may require adding additional team members if some dynamics of the deal changes. Some potential add-ons could be a contractor, a co-borrower or co-signer, or maybe even an eligible FHA gift giver.

On first base you will have your loan/mortgage officer. This team member will be responsible for initiating and guiding you through your loan approval and origination process. On second base you will have your home inspector. Your home inspector will be responsible for looking over your home's physical condition from top to bottom. The home inspector's job is to discover any latent or patent defects on behalf of the buyer. The accumulated results will enlighten and enable all contractual parties to effectively resolve this period of due diligence with precision. Be mindful that it's not uncommon for a home inspector to recommend further assessment of a discovered defect by a specialized contractor. Do not allow this to deter nor discourage you. It's a home inspector's job to uncover, expose and document their findings via a report to the buyer. On third base you will have your title company. The title company is responsible for the transference of an insured title to the new owner. They can also assist with ordering land surveys and establishes a precise and thorough settlement statement. This statement includes the breakdown and accuracy of all line items, loan figures, prorations, credits, debits and title fees to complete the closing.

All team members are important but not perfect. Any team member has the potential to drop the ball. I can't stress enough how important it is to acquire a seasoned real estate team. An experienced agent is always on guard when looking out for any indications of threats to the loan origination. Your real estate agent is the team's captain; but stay mindful that situations may arise. These situations can mimic an ambush and totally fall outside of the agent's control. Having an experienced and focused team can present a very low probability of this happening.

Chapter 7

DOWN PAYMENT AND CLOSING COSTS ASSISTANCE

As a real estate professional, the most prevalent question that I'm asked is about assistance with down payment and closing costs. Let's take a closer look to clarify and understand their purpose. Your down payment will typically be your portion of the loan value-- determined by your lender and loan type. This percentage can differ per loan type and loan conditions. Most common loan types will have a standard percentage less the loan to value (LTV). VA loans will typically carry a 100% LTV, but you will still incur a funding fee. FHA insured loans typically have a minimum down payment of 3.5% of the loan value. Conventional loans can carry up to a standard 20% down payment.

Your closing costs will be the total amount needed to close on your home. Your total closing costs will include your down payment. Closing costs also includes a plethora of pre-disclosed charges and fees such as loan origination fees, escrows, commissions, title charges and many more. So it's a great idea to keep in touch with your lender to assist you with "good faith" estimates up until the day of your official closing.

A buyer should always be ahead of the game by having accessible funds that covers their down payment and closing costs. A buyer is encouraged to have at least 3% of the sales price of the home in savings. This can also give the lender a better sense of security that the buyer will be able to close. Strategizing is key and simply being prepared is best. Having a great lender on the team is advantageous. A great lender can help a buyer by providing good faith numbers and figures based upon their price range and interest rate.

Negotiating down payment and closing costs with the seller is a good way to offset these costs. It's very important for you and your real estate agent to sit down and discuss offer strategies. Most sellers are willing to assist buyers with down payment and closing costs assistance with a well-balanced offer. The offer should be attractive enough to encourage the seller to assist the buyer. We must keep in mind that a seller wants to sell their home and the buyer wants to purchase it.

We certainly can't forget to discuss down payment and closing costs assistance programs and how they work. A buyer should always inquire about these programs and grants. Many lenders who specialize in first time homebuyers will have some type of assistance and/or products to offer. This assistance can be "in-house" which means through the lender or it can also be administered through local grant-based housing counselors. You can also check with your real estate agent to see if they know of any resources that may be applicable in all regards. These programs and grants are not a "one size fits all." Due to income limits, demographics, debt-to-income ratio and credit issues, many homebuyers may not qualify for these down payments and closing costs assistance programs.

 Some down payment and closing costs assistance programs have classroom requirements whether online or in person. The vast majority of these grants are forgivable but not all. Your lender should be able to tell you if you're a likely candidate for this type of assistance. Be sure to discuss this option with your lender and real estate agent to see if you qualify and what assistance may be currently available.

Chapter 8

MORTGAGE LOAN PRODUCTS

Mortgage loan products are typically created "in house" by the lender. These products are typically incentivized and geared towards first time homebuyer and even mortgage refinance candidates. They're designed to assist an eligible first time home buyer with down payment and or closing costs assistance. Eligible refinance mortgagors are typically incentivized with lower interest rates and reduced mortgage payments. Like any business, mortgage lending must stay competitive, reputable and reliable.

It's truly just as beneficial to a lender to carry loan products for eligible first time home buyers as it is for buyers that need them. Buyers come to lenders with various financial situations and limitations. Lenders who carry mortgage loan products can certainly edge out the competition. Having the ability to offer a first time homebuyer in need of a little financial assistance some monetary relief could change the game entirely. The underlying objective is to fuel the American Dream of Homeownership and to keep communities beautiful and desirable with homeowners.

The vast majority of these mortgage loan products will already have the primary qualifications spelled out. Don't be shy when asking your lender about these products and grants. Many mortgage loan products are created "in house" but can be provided through local housing and counseling agencies as well.

23

Chapter 9

LET'S BUY A HOUSE

The pathway that leads to your dream home has been established. It's now time to hit the road! A buyer's pre-approved loan amount will be the primary factor in determining what they're able to purchase. Once pre-approved, it's a great idea to sit down with your real estate agent and discuss this pre-approved amount and loan type in comparison to what you're looking for in a home. The initial discussion before setting out on your home search should consist of the following:

- ⇨ buyer's loan amount

- ⇨ current market condition

- ⇨ strategic planning

- ⇨ an overview of how the home search will look

A buyer should have a realistic idea of what they have the ability to purchase. This briefing should happen before setting out to look for the dream home.

The Lender could also be included in this discussion. Loan officers are typically pretty good at helping a buyer understand the value of their pre-approval also. Lenders have the ability to provide buyers with "good faith" estimates and mortgage worksheets based off their loan amount. These estimates give the buyer a snapshot of their anticipated mortgage. The worksheet is an itemized breakdown of their total loan and all fees including principal, interest, taxes and insurance. The buyer should always be top priority. A buyer should be made to feel welcomed in assisting their real estate agent with the home search. Many buyers will already be aware of some must haves and some definite deal breakers.

It is very important for the team to stay on the same page and the rapport remains pleasant. Things could go really bad if a buyer feels disregarded or unimportant. Real estate agents must remain patient and mindful that "true" first time homebuyers will need to be educated throughout the process. Many first time homebuyers have memories of negative experiences with previous agents or simply have misconstrued visions of how the home buying search actually works. So again, real estate agents-- do not skip the consultations. Always discuss the client's financial ability in comparison to their needs and the current state of the real estate market. An agent should always make themselves accessible to their buyers. Oftentimes buyers will have questions and will need their agent's help to understand the process. There are many reasons why an agency can break down or fall apart. We should always remember to keep our client's best interest as priority and maintain integrity throughout the journey.

Chapter 10

ENERGY EFFICIENCY

You've now purchased your dream home and you're feeling amazing! As a new homeowner, there is so much anticipation and so many visions centered on theme, décor and comfort. We're all aware of traditional improvements such as painting, flooring upgrades, contemporary fixtures and curb appeal adding value to a home. Your home can literally save you money all year round, improve comfort and add more value instantly. Let's take a trip through your home and explore the potential.

Energy efficient and smart homes have become the norm with regard to efficiency and convenience. Many tend to think energy efficient and smart upgrades are either too costly or not really worth it at all. Energy efficient and smart homes are just regular homes with wireless, eco and energy upgrades. The upgrades allow better control and manage energy usage for increased comfort and access. As energy prices continue to soar and technology continues to thrive, these upgrades have become necessary and beneficial to buyers.

When speaking of smart homes, smart hubs can certainly improve the quality in all regards. Linking appliances, utilities, access and lighting to smart hubs can provide the ultimate convenience. Smart hub devices allow homeowners to control and monitor installed smart devices via Wi-Fi. This can be done remotely by way of Wi-Fi enabled apps. Controlling of our level of comfort, convenience and security within our homes is a game changer. A homeowner could simply convert to LED lighting throughout their home. LED lighting provides brighter and safer light which consumes far less energy than any other lighting that has come before it. Incorporating energy efficient appliances could really decrease the monthly electric bill also.

These appliances are typically labeled as "Energy efficient" somewhere on the unit or packaging. Additional upgrades and improvements that can be made includes-- installing smart thermostats, sealing windows to prevent drafts inside the home, adding low flow toilets and adding low E windows where needed. The price of energy efficient upgrades will enable you to pay yourself back over time with cost-savings, comfort and quality.

We can certainly go on and on highlighting energy efficient and smart home upgrades and benefits that will equate to huge savings on your utility bills over time. The savings can potentially be applied to the principal balance on your mortgage; this may ultimately result in an earlier payoff. The next time you're in a home improvement store or shopping online, take a moment to view some energy efficient appliances and smart home devices to gauge ideas that may be suitable for your home. Adding energy efficient and smart home upgrades to your home will have you appreciating the fact that your new home is appreciating in value!

Chapter II

DEFINITIONS

1. **First time home buyer** — Someone who is purchasing their very first home or a buyer who hasn't owned a home for at least three years.

2. **Pre-Approval** — A statement of confirmation given to the buyer once the loan officer evaluates and approves all information within the mortgage application. The lender renders a decision and discloses the amount the buyer may borrow for the home purchase.

3. **Conventional Loan** — These are home loans that are not backed by the government and can typically require a higher down payment. This loan type can be more appealing to a seller as it require less paperwork and offer more monetary flexibility. Conventional loans can be conforming or non-conforming.

4. **FHA Loan** — This loan type is government and FHA insured. This loan is more appealing to a low to moderate income borrower. This loan type typically requires a lower down payment and lower credit score to qualify than a conventional loan. The FHA loan process can be more time consuming given additional requirements and restrictions per the government.

5. **FHA Gift** — A contribution of cash or equity from an approved donor with no expectation of repayment. This option is typically offered when a borrower requires assistance with their down payment or closing costs.

6. **Fixed Rate Mortgage** — A mortgage type with a fixed interest rate for the life of the loan.

7. **Adjustable Rate Mortgage (ARM)** — A mortgage type in which the initial rate could vary throughout the life of the loan. The fluctuation would be contingent upon the financial index associated with that loan.

8.   **Community Reinvestment Act (CRA)** — A federal law enacted in 1977 to encourage depository institutions to meet the credit needs of low-to-moderate income neighborhoods.

9.   **Interest Rate** — Is the amount of interest or percentage rate due per period as a proportion of the amount lent. In laymen terms it's just simply the cost of money for that specific transaction.

10. **Debt–to–Income–Ration** — This formula calculates the total amount of money earned by the borrower from month to month versus what's owed. This formula does factor in the anticipated mortgage as a debit also.

11. **Loan–to–Value (LTV)** — A measure comparing the amount of your mortgage with the appraised value of the property. The higher your down payment, the lower your LTV ratio.

12. **Down Payment** — a said amount of money a buyer is required to pay as part of the purchasing process. The down payment represents a percentage of the total purchase price.

13. **Closing Costs** — These are general fees for services and expenses required to finalize a mortgage.

14. **Down Payment & Closing Costs Assistance** — This is standard financial assistance granted to the borrower to help cover their portion of their required costs to finalize the loan. This assistance can come from a multitude of sources. Some sources could include a seller, a gift giver, a first time home buyer assistance entity, the lending institution itself or other.

15. **Co-Signer** — A person who agrees to take responsibility and/or take over the mortgage if the borrower stops paying.

16. **Co-Borrower** — someone who applies for a loan with another borrower. All borrowers have full responsibility for payments.

17. **Principal/Interest/Taxes/Insurance (PITI)** — This is what a mortgage is comprised of--some borrowers with larger down payments along with stronger credit scores may request to pay their taxes and insurance independently.

18. **Mortgage Underwriting** — This is the process a lender uses to determine borrower eligibility when applying for a mortgage loan. This is a very thorough and in depth process.

19. **Loan Commitment** — Your lender has formally approved you for the loan.

20. **Clear to Close (C2C)** — this is music to everyone's ears. This simply means that all requirements and conditions have been met to close on your mortgage.

21. **Amortization Schedule** — this is a simple breakdown of your mortgage over the life of the loan in equal payments.

22. **Closing Day** — This is the day where ownership of the property officially transfers to the buyer. This day is also known as settlement day or the day of settlement.

Chapter 12

CREDIT TIPS

1.   The current FICO range is 300-850. Although the standard range is 720, it's a great idea to shoot for the very best credit score possible. Please stay mindful that your credit score will determine the cost of credit that's loaned to you. Creditworthiness is certainly a term that you would want to become partners with. Everyone should understand how priceless and beneficial this term is. One could certainly enjoy a much better life financially by simply having upstanding creditworthiness.

2.   Order a copy of your free credit report. An individual is granted one free credit report annually from each of the three major consumer reporting agencies. You can request a credit score along with your free report but this option does require a modest fee. You can now begin to check your credit report for any errors such as grammatical, typos, identity, aliases, addresses and other. Credit history impacts and makes up approximately 15% of your credit score.

3.   It's a good idea to read your credit report often. Many people can dispute and resolve minor incorrections themselves. If too many derogatory and negative items are discovered, it would be encouraged for one to enlist the assistance of a credit expert.

4.   Pay all bills on time and consider using automatic bill pay along with having your paycheck enrolled in direct deposit.

5.   Do not max out credit cards and do not open several new accounts all at once. Try to charge smaller amounts that can be paid back on time. If you're carrying high credit card balances, pay them down. It's ideal to keep your credit card balances at or below 30% of the total limit. It would be an even better idea to keep them as close to 0% of the total limit without closing them. Outstanding credit card balances impacts and makes up approximately 30% of your credit score.

6.   Know the difference between revolving accounts and installment accounts. An example of a revolving account is a credit card account. An example of an installment account is an auto loan. Revolving accounts can be credit boosters if used responsibly. Although revolving credit are great boosters, it's still not wise to have very many of them in relation to installment accounts. The type of credit on your credit report impacts and makes up approximately 10% of your credit score.

7.   Many people believe closing credit card accounts once paid off will help their credit score. Maintaining healthy credit card accounts such as paying as agreed and maintaining very low balances is best.

8.   There are hard inquiries, soft inquiries and self-inquiries when it comes to credit hits and pulls. Hard inquiries are also known as hard pulls and soft inquiries are also known as soft pulls. Both options can remain on your credit for approximately two years. Soft pulls are typically not seen by other viewers other than yourself and may not even affect your credit at all. Hard pulls typically are used when it's decision making time to grant a person credit. Self pulls doesn't present any hits and doesn't affect credit at all. Inquiries impacts and makes up approximately 10% of your credit score.

9.   Try not to miss any payments. Typically it can take up to twenty four months to restore credit with just one late payment. Even worse is that the amount of the default will not change the ramifications. Please stay mindful that it's very important to pay your bills and stay on top of what's on your credit report. Payment history impacts and makes up approximately 35% or your credit score.

10.   Secured credit cards can be a major help to someone who wants to build or re-build credit. They work similar to a debit card in that your individual funds are involved. The issuing bank will grant you a credit card with a credit limit. That bank will use your funds to secure the debt in any case of default. Cash deposits are required from the borrower by the bank when seeking this option.

ABOUT THE AUTHOR

Ricky L. Hopkins, Sr. is an award-winning real estate broker from St. Louis, Missouri. He currently owns and manages A-List, Realtors® LLC located in north St. Louis County. He has been a member of the National, Missouri and St. Louis Association of Realtors® since 2007. He received his real estate education from the Coldwell-Banker School of Real Estate, Career Education Systems and Meramec College. It was also at Meramec College where he received his residential appraisal education and mentoring. Ricky Sr. teamed up with Central Bank of St. Louis in Ferguson, Missouri where they held free credit repair, first time home buyer and financial literacy workshops from 2015-2017.

Ricky Sr. continued to direct his real estate experience into the community. He teamed up with the St. Louis Association of Realtors® and Rebuilding Together St. Louis from 2016-2020 as he co-led their Community Engagement Committee. This committee was designed to locate homes with the neediest repairs and repair them absolutely free for the homeowner. The homeowners were typically elderly, disabled, retired-military or just homeowners unable to do it themselves. He went on to become Board Chairman of the Real Estate Housing Assistance fund (RHAF).

Ricky Sr. earned his At Home with Diversity designation (AHWD) from the National Association of Realtors® in 2021. This designation complements the community engagement efforts given it is all centered on equity and inclusion within communities. He continues his community engagement efforts now working as a director on the St. Louis Zoo's Executive Board of Directors. Ricky Sr. was very instrumental throughout the St. Louis north county region in advocating Proposition Z. This proposition passed and provides additional tax funding for the St. Louis Zoo's Wild

Care Park. The Wild Care Park is scheduled to open in early 2027 in North St. Louis County. He continues to teach and mentor upcoming real estate agents and dedicates much of his time giving back to the surrounding communities where he lives and work.

DEDICATION

I would like to first thank my mother Ola Mae Hopkins and my wife Rochelle Hopkins. My mom and wife are everything to me. My mother didn't miss a beat while raising my brothers and myself as a single parent. I could certainly write a book on my mom alone. She continues to take good care of us through her unwavering love, support and tireless dedication. God could not have given me a better mom. My wife keeps me sharp and happy. She's not only my high school sweetheart but one of the hardest working women I know. We are headed towards reaching a major milestone — thirty years of marriage.

To my grandmother who passed in 2007 — certainly words alone can't express the appreciation I have for her. The impact she left upon my life is infinite. Her life lessons are a part of my daily decisions and she will forever dwell with me. To my older brothers and protectors Robert and Rodney Hopkins. We remain very close to this day and they have always made sure that I was safe, well cared for and sheltered. As a child, I was one of the youngest in my entire family. Everyone always treated me like a baby and kept their eyes on me.

To my fabulous aunts Renae, Paralia, and Quinzola (deceased) who served as mothers to me also. They were always there for me, given our family was so close. I appreciate them so much for loving me and being there when mom was working. They still treat me like a baby even to this day. When I look back over my life, I've been truly blessed with a great family. I would like to send a special acknowledgement to Mr. Paul Kenner (deceased). He's not my biological grandfather but the only grandfather I know. He loved my grandmother and took care of the household. He was a handyman and took me out as a youngster to do odd jobs for residents and friends in the neighborhood. He was very knowledgeable, trustworthy and fun-loving. The things he taught have certainly manifested into my acumen. I would like to send a special shout out to all my cousins, our childhood would not have been the same without one another. We were all so close and I can visualize us playing at school and throughout the neighborhoods.

Last but certainly not least, I would like to thank my father Lige Higgins, Jr. and all my children. Ricky L. Hopkins, Jr., Ryan Hopkins, Richelle Hopkins and Rick Hopkins (deceased) I love you all. There's not a day that goes by, that I don't think of you all. I lost many family members; but I have many left and I'm grateful. I try my hardest to be the very best for my children. This world is far different today versus when I was a child. As I look back over my life and see how far God has brought me, I can't help but to keep going. I couldn't possibly name everyone individually who has made a difference in my life, so I am offering a universal Thank you -to any and everyone who has brought any value to my life.

ACKNOWLEDGEMENTS

I would also like to acknowledge Barry UpChurch. Barry is a very good friend and real estate colleague who has always believed in me and keeps me encouraged. He led our real estate association's Community Engagement efforts. He's well educated and very bright along with being a visionary. He continues to work in the communities as a national and local Officer with ReBuilding Together. ReBuilding Together is a national nonprofit. They provide repairs to homes in significant disrepair. Their goal is to create safe and healthy homes for the elderly, disabled, veterans and homeowners who are just unable to repair their homes. I believe he and I were brought together strategically by God to do this work. We've achieved and accomplished many things together.

I want to send a special acknowledgement to Rochelle Hopkins, LaMonica D. Evans, Sinita Wells, Tricia Key and my A-List Agents who hold me accountable. Last but certainly not least, special acknowledgement to my lord and savior Jesus Christ for always coming to see about me.

www.ingramcontent.com/pod-product-compliance
Lightning Source LLC
Chambersburg PA
CBHW051338150726
47997CB00004B/1520